Witness

Heather Brett

'Witness'
is published by
Windows Publications 2015
2 Loreto Wood
Cavan, Co Cavan

ISBN 0-9551721-8-7 / 9789551721-8-2

www.windowspublicationsanddesign.com

The cover is taken from 'The Wheel of Fortune'
by Edward Burne-Jones.

Witness

Heather Brett

Acknowledgements

I would like to acknowledge 'Ghosts of the Faithful Departed' by David Creedon where 'Oh Ireland' was first published; Poetic Republic E Book for 'Contract' and Live Encounters Literary Magazine Online for 'Testament', 'Witness' & 'Bankrupt'.

A heartfelt thank-you to all who helped make this book possible - Noel, Anne, Philip & Catriona for all the reading...and my friends at Blacks Printers for everything!
To Cavan County Council for the 2015 Professional Development Award.
A special thanks to Cavan Arts & Heritage Offices who supported several projects where some of these poems were the outcome.

Also by Heather Brett

Abigail Brown (Salmon 1991)
The Touch Maker (Alternative Press 1996)
Green Monkey, ***travelling*** *(*Bluechrome 2006*)*

Contents

For my beautiful grandchildren,
Cory, Michael, Ashlee & Eireann
and my wonderful sisters Lorraine & Anne

Without a family, man,
alone in the world,
trembles with the cold.

Andre Maurois

Art

open
fingerspread the spine
inhale newness
white as a cocaine crease
this fathomless breach
into which all of me tumbles
headfirst
skin left, snagged on a paperclip
edge, an overcoat hung, still wearing
the shape of its owner.

Miles away I come to
resurface
the words caught in my throat
like a cormorant
fishing

The Time to Exit has Expired

It's all grey
especially from the vantage point of hindsight
the lighting, the concrete, the car park
even the situation…
the impatience in you.
The Now Syndrome, plundered.
Wait.
All I ever said was *wait.*

Bankrupt

I eat the last of the white peaches from Sedona.
Delicate inlay of texture and taste.
The sun hasn't quite reached my window yet
but the patio is alive; tiny prehistoric,
long-thin-tailed lizards that jack
and pump themselves on the brickwork;
bees hover and burrow in the lemon rose
of the cacti
and stripped agave amid the creosote
pushes its spikes skyward,
pierces the shadow of a turkey vulture,
wings outstretched, feathers spread,
rifling the sizzling air.
Glint of blue-green-black butterfly flap,
crickets that pulse and trill from the milkweed.

I think of that particular point where one stops
watching, stops listening,
folds back the formed word on the tongue,
stops feeling:
and I wonder how long I've been sitting here
a study in loss, but breathing.

Lent

Soon there will only be a sense
of the road dwindling into the distance…
the swans, the dead fish all pointers
towards emotional turmoil.

This week, still of penance, of washed feet
and unholy cartels - what a time to reinvent
myself, to resurrect the lifeless,
dust off the pale and brittle bones:

White horses chomp on your
beach; a shore line beckons like the
refuge it isn't. Daylight dwindles, and with it
any good reason to stay.

Daughter…

above the sink, on the windowsill
I have placed your photograph.

At least once a day, I stand here
gazing in on you.

That one time I dreamt of you,
you were wearing sky blue,

your hair a blond sheaf
falling: you turned towards me

and your smile was knowing.
Everything and all that we are.

Each day, I tell you how sorry I am,
notice how your voice is fading.

I only moved here last September,
I still paint a little, still write.

Why is it that can't I hear you?
It's like you're behind

a wall of thick glass,
a snow globe, where you're always twenty,

always smiling.
Is it me? Have I stopped listening?

I put the knives away,
fold over the dishcloth.

Visitor

So, death came.
Stole silently and without warning
one of yours,
hooked a supposedly black talon
through a shirt tab
and disappeared,
the remnants of your family
strewn over the carpet, the garden
the street and beyond.
You, bristling each time someone spoke
in case the response wasn't warranted
removed from it all, yet in the thick of it,
knowing nothing, everything.

We are all so correct now
I can't reach for fear of leading,
you can't accept for fear of falling,
both of us skirting thc issucs,
dodging the fallout
retreating.

Nothing will ever be the same again,
but we'll go on
a little more hardened,
a lot more prepared.

Instinct

for my son, Greg

Morning, early, a last damp breath
then an instant of startling clarity
before the burnish
that slightest of blush on the backdrop;
a promise.

My son, the man:
always the blonde child
laughing from the water.
Always the boy
I cradled. *Pietà.*

The last breath.
Dusk swallows delicately
all the birdsong,
the flowers stretch,
this one red-bronze day.

Waning

Darkness is an entity
we breathe him in and exhale
plumes of light.
Outside, the moon pearls,
indigo clouds shift.

Your heart is too big for me, I cannot wear it
or shape it smaller
or bundle it up and parcel it on.
There are some skins
we definitely can’t grow into.

But just for a moment
we walked this road together
our path sunkissed as a memory,
hayseeds in our hair and our time
blessed.

I Can't See It But I Know It's There

The dream lists towards the subconscious,
keels over and pours into memory,
spills through a latticework grill
oils a cog, revolves.
Illusionary teeth mesh.

The shadow of a sparrow lands
on the shadow of my roof.
Glare of sunlight, flare of
little shadow wings
searing burnt, orange, black.

The Theory of Everything

A wild little tiger shares my garden;
she comes early
when dew dampens,
slicks the docken leaves
mottles the concrete block;
or late when the sky's bruises quicken
to leak indigo shadows,
the horizon already a dirty mauve.
She stares her taut stare
iris elliptical, all gold and jade
and her perfect little mouth parts
to hiss a warning,
prongs of sharp eye teeth
glint: pale pink and tiny tongue.
I have never touched her.
Never stroked her achromatic pelt,
tabby stripes,
the grey its own complement.
She owns everything, allows me to be.

Premonition

Beget. Begin. Be.
Nuclei form
veined
and bloodwashed.
Anchors.
The womb fills.
Fluid whispers, fears,
part genetic fingerprint,
part future.
These are the sins no x-ray sees.
The fraying begins
before he is born
and all his life
he is unravelling,
until one long night
around dusk perhaps,
the thread runs out,
the canopy, the fabric, rent.

A Businessman Takes the Night Air

parc st cloud tulips
ragged edges rare and waving
a whole fused tilt towards mirth.
Now I can place you
in a different frame, askew:
the suit, the hair, the jousting lance
hastiludes of modern commerce
and concrete verse
and still appreciate the dusk
the smell of earth
openness

Alternative

I don’t even remember the cold.
Only that there was space,
nothing got in the way of floor,
ceiling, floor:
linear squared.

Whatever happened - happened on the
periphery.

But perhaps I have imagined even this;
Spars of minerals thrust
and somewhere DNA molecules
turn and lock,
wave after wave of history
mushrooms,
rushes and spills
searching for it’s own level

When

When the wide mouth of loss
opens,
steady yourself:
When the dark earth splits apart
and there's a rent in the air,
steel yourself:
When space is humbled and the
shadows group –
hold fast.
The spirit is wounded and has
cause to grieve,
only hurt can follow.
Give in to the anguish,
lay down your cheek to the soil,
claw grass and soft moss by the clump,
know a cool resistance in stone.
And when all of this has happened,
when the coin is folded over and palmed
and the last clear raindrop fallen,
find somewhere, the image of a hilltop
lengths that go gentle to grass,
a tree perhaps, where the shade is
deep and purpled
and step in.

Fringe

The edges of the lake
froze here.
Ripples solidified,
the swans, the reeds, the trees
all a still white.

Miles away,
an ocean.
Snow absorbed by wave.
You skimmed stones flat as dollars
silvered by the moon.

In the cold here,
in a bright, almost electric whiteness
a single shadow is highlighted.

That crumpled sea,
a sense of ebb and flow,
give and take, wish and want,
and lastly - less and always, loss.

Witness

for Anne Marie

Bay-willow on the turn;
the leaves levitate
ablaze within their redness:
the flowers spent, soft pods split,
yield a froth of silk to whiteness,
to tiny spiders,
to the sharpening wind.

I take my grief to the stones,
lay down my sorrow on timeless grass
ease this weight of loss;
address the leaves in the listening trees,
submit to the waiting green,
enfold a shadowed expanse of sky,
burrow, in cool and porous rock.

Stone remembers: holds tight within
the scent of coming rain,
the frivolous and fickle winds
layer after layer laid, bone on shell on skin:
Fireweed and forest: longing, loss and give
cellular ages of existence
under the ceaseless and alabaster moon.

Transvestite, seated

After Diane Arbus

There are points to be considered here:
light and highlights,
horizontals, straight and narrows,
that levelled, complaisant gaze:
the cross on the tee
of transvestite,
the hangbeam of the y in boy.

The mantle leads,
right-angled neck against relaxed shoulder
or the other way about. Thigh to shy knee,
the sheen of nylon stocking.
A scribbled strip of edge along the seat:
Black patent shoe.
Ruled flooring, tongue and lip of groove.

I cannot sleep.
Beams across the ceiling underline it.

Familiar

Early and a thick fog
nestles either side of Mc Shane's Pass -
as if every spruce and blade of grass
were giving up the ghost
white whispers
ratting out O'Neill survivors
from near five centuries ago.

My grandson plays some game
of thrones, battlescarred defenders
of an old and mythical place
land cut and divided, brother
against brother, magicians and
religion, dirt, poverty and dragons.
Nothing changes, I tell him.

Cinnabar Moth and the Messenger

When the grass is this long
I rise early,
metallic rasp of pheasant,
insistent muffle
of a collared, cooing wood pigeon:
trillings and twittering
placed so lightly in the
backdrop of the settling day;
the whole morning a-quiver
slowly and surely balancing,
bracing and flexing to enfold
these many hours ahead.

Grass cool and damp
springs, clover purples
between my toes, bruised
and cream chrysanthemums.
My friend the scientist says
that for every 10,000 stems
there is only one four-leafed clover;
some odds then, luck to be plucked
at random:
and I think of the travelling blacksmith,
his gift of a horseshoe and one nail
that I toted back to the kingdom,
Gower and Franklin on my mind.

Light floods the sky, a tint of yellow promise,
something aqua rising.
Ragwort stalks the garden, laden
with inch-long, voracious caterpillars,
black and amber larvae
black and red in their formal wear,
evening cape and gothic collar.
A messenger lands,
cocks his head and his eyes hold.
Whatever comes, he says,
won't be pleasant:
Can't be undone.

Canker

This hush
if left unchecked
will spread,
fan out and seep
on, relentless.
And before you know it
someone, reminiscent of yourself perhaps,
will rise
white haired, dead eyed:
fold herself up
into a tight synthetic shroud
and exit offstage

On the other hand -
checked -
the very air could alter,
minute particles of colour
wing home,
implode inside an iris
and gather,
pinkly skimming
on the cheekbone
break cover
to tug upwards
the waiting smile.

Issues and Electric Kisses

stares
a thousand words deep:
the space between us
traversed and spiked,
charged with differences; the sum
of all we have been, and all that we are,
raw and eager.
Warily we press fingers into flesh, flinch
at the burn, press harder,
ablaze and unravelling.

But odysseys take their toll: masks slip and
cracks widen: only the husk remains.

Bittersweet, the woodsmoke rises,
charred skin and hearts, criss-crossed
cicatrix of protection; living amulet,
de-sensitised and immune.
Nerve endings are frazzled and only, only just,
the shroud spared, the winding sheet marred.
It folds around us, familiar, content
while emptiness lingers,
swells in the sterile air.

Marked

Winter, and we close ranks,
huddle inside in the stale, central
heated air that lies over everything
like a thermal wave, a long dry sigh.
The waiting is a constant
moon waning, blessings aired
and recounted, time and time again.
Penance.

Age steps into the house like a landlord.
We know he owns us,
doff our cap and offer a sacrifice
of wellbeing.
It visits us all. This grey, pervading ask.
A house can stay the winter,
pale acceptance, a hushed bribe;
rooms hollowed out, space left
bereft and afraid,
alert for the slightest sign of warmth.

Kelly Angel Dream Theme 2001

I have this scenario
where I bundle you up
in my big brown suede coat
yes - the one I got the green paint on
and carry you – yes carry you -
down to the doctors -
the young one that even you might fancy
and he smiles and he makes you well
and you don't die.

But this isn't a gameshow
with multiple choices or help from the
audience:
you're gone
and that one truth deadens everything.
My best hope is that Joey Dunlop
stops outside the morgue for you,
smiles his shy smile
waits while you climb on behind him
while you cling to him my lovely girl
and you ride off towards the horizon
on some silver 850cc dream machine,
white smoke from the exhaust
making tiny phut phut clouds
in a turquoise sky.

Chinese Walls

here
where we pretend
everything is open,
small sounds stretch between us,
curve out their whispers
in the mottled air
to burrow themselves
in the long day

In real time,
where the air has already changed,
redolent of loss,
we see the same things
and continue on regardless.
Another past,
another pattern.
And the night knows, roughly
the shape of things to come.

There are many ways to be,
many ways to brace yourself
camouflage the open wound,
dodge the poised blade;
and always, always, ignore
the stain of mildew, spreading

The Crypt at Castle Saunderson

Bronze hawker dragonflies loiter and hang
in the sunlit midair.
Warmed grass preens, stretching
its hold on the summer.
The light settles easy here, pale brick
and bird song, textured trunk and
offered shadow;
and all the witnessing leaves…
a green hush reigns
while cold stonework sweats,
damp and dew descend,
tears of time to moisten the dark.
Here collected, lies love and longing.
Here collected, lies solitude.
Here collected are all the remains of life
human and humble,
in a time tarnished pale lead box,
consolingly cool to the touch.

Claim

You arrived early on
Nothing to herald the summons
no introductions to speak of
but an uneasy acceptance
of what, by all accounts
must've been yours for the taking

I remember you
hoarding the silences,
setting aside those intervals of space
where others couldn't go.
Transparent days overrun with sleep.
Long empty nights all your own.

It's all relative. We bear witness
to the consummation of things
just or unjust;
Our whole lives out on loan.
An indelible scrawl in a ledger,
a definitive debt to be paid.

Codicil

we lob
musings, memories, music
mindful of the trappings, the stage, the cast.
It's as if yours is the script
I've been forever reading, your voice
mine, only different,
DNA, reference, equi-distant
viewpoints albeit perhaps,
from different corners.
Whatever, mon chéri,
a new sea sings in my ear
low notes
that only the sirens hear.
As the moon halts the tide
on a Dalkey beach
a new watermark is revealed,
new depths breached.

Flint

Although already abandoned,
it took time before I understood,
time before I recognised indifference

and an even longer time
before I could shape and name the thing
overall

and I wondered, if,
averse myself to embrace wholly,
had I somehow known

that these roots would never bind me,
would never tether me to this partitioned land;
that this soil would never sing in my blood:

Perhaps I had arrived reserved,
unable - *afraid* to invest,
the heartstrings already severed

and the word home, merely myth.

II

But for those I took the measure of
there was a gain
a marvel to witness colonialism-

the regime alive and well and residing
across the border, along with a stiff salute
and loose Tory tactics…

the clones, the divide, the abhorrence
of all things not in their pigeon hole,
not dotted or crossed or -

heaven forbid - not *straight.*
That uncanny trait to call a spade a spade
as if it were something admirable,

something in our genes like green eyes.
I can't breathe there, the air gives
me heartburn, and I fear for the multitude,

for the lost class, a *now* generation
of ignored offspring, migrant kids,
nomads

Things Left

…blonde reeds breathe
by the lake’s edge
water that won’t quite
give up its sky
lies quiet.

swans fly out each morning
return and go again
five, sometimes seven
never an equal number

I exist here
tend to my life
keep track of loose threads
any empty hours
longings

winter’s last grasp
slipping,
offering its blue throat
to a patient sun.

Oh Ireland

for Katie and Margaret McAleese

The second leaving,
a Spring day in March
and a railway station in the north.
and the very last time you see your sister.
She gets an hour off from the mill
to say goodbye forever.
Then Belfast, the docks, the pier awash with tears.
A boat to Southampton
for the liner out.
You're on your own now,
the first leaving back
when you fell for the Protestant,
threw your hat in with the other crowd,
broke free from every sort of rope
that bound convention.

March sea, the cheaper fare.
A full week moored to your cabin
while the ocean swells,
falls back,
waves tilt and thicken with ice.
Ireland behind you,
the Atlantic below
and a new found coastline beckons.

Those were the years of telegraphs
and distance,
thin airmails and funerals,
snow drifts, and lamps for the darkness.
All the leaving and the waiting,
to go or get there or even return,
two sides of the same tossed coin
a silver bright half-crown,
or perhaps, that unfamiliar dollar.

At Multyfarnham

for Salvador, Diarmuid, John, Richard and Joe

Enclosed here
this past while,
there's been space to
watch things: grey
seep through lapis lazuli
the group and chaos
of crows
and how the mist hangs sometimes
in the dull midair.
Books hunker on almost every surface.
Somewhere, water continuously dreams:
Embroidered with canticle and psalm
the days dilate and shrink,
bloom again.
A collective peace stirs,
nudges a tiny opening in the
heart; enters.

The Formation of Ice Crystals

It's early, before nine
and minus five in Omagh.
Then a side road
over the flattened hills
towards Fermanagh

Rime frost follows the fog,
frozen air weighted,
a halo around every tree
inhaling light,
a white lei along every branch
a caught breath over every bush.

This hush has stalked me
for weeks,
cold numbing of rehearsed words,
ice crystals on my tongue,
chilling my speech.
A chance to acclimatise
adjust to all things cold,
The future bleak,
bereft and abundant
in one and the same breath.

When I said space,
I really meant distance.

Matriarch

for Lily

I have known you a full decade;
have been included in your arms wide embrace
awed by the reach of your heart,
soothed by your soft, encouraging speak.
Minder of all small things, a past enfolds,
falls around us, woven, a tapestry sewn,
stories stitched and sutured,
the yarns and silk as one -
'*show me your hurt, girl, and I'll show you mine...*'
These are the days of our autumn
threads of gold, found leaf of russet and
amber flake
kindness your unspoken currency
acceptance your unstinting reach:

Friend, it's your hand on the tiller,
perpetual thimble on your thumb.

Testament

for Jack Keyes

This was the year of the flood.
Even the curious Kennypottle, alive and
running away with itself
ventured out over the road,
sandbags left slumped and dreaming
against the doors on Railway Street.
And I was thinking of beginnings and
endings; how we *stay* this wondrous road,
the countless that walk unseen beside us
the multitude that have yet to come -
each and every one of us seeking solace,
the right to be,
belong,
become.

This place of archaic stone splinters,
fragments the past, the here and now,
us: In a March light fog jostles the skyline
mutes the amber grass
and in the thickening air long dead echoes
rise: warm slick of salted wave,
ancient hush from a shroud of ice.
Cushion moss glows ochre green,
carpets stone and boulder, native ash
compliments the tiny purple orchid
shelters hare, wheatear and moth;

muffles the absent call of fallow deer
Green Man of the keep.

This outcropped earth cradles;
ancient field, valley and cairn combine, give
up the clearings to our dead;
a witness made of every bramble,
blade of grass an offered prayer.
Here is ceremony and peace,
a chant in every fractured rock
hum of want from the mirrored lough,
fall of vibrant light,
where portal stone, chalk hill and grave
align within
wait out this fragile trust
in a perfect linear reach to a solstice sun.

Notturno

The pianist closes his eyes,
inclines his head, aslant,
aware of an inner sound
a chord, born within the wood
a note clean and pure
tempered breath of felt and steel and tone
a chord, at one with the opening air

My son joins him, moves
soundlessly, all eyes except mine, blind.
My girl too, steps into the frame and the
pianist tenses, eyes closed,
aware of a soft restlessness,
the displacement of my heart,
hurt.

Absence

I see them often, those dead men
walking, shuffling along the road
heads bent, shoulders bunched as
if weighed down by the whole uneven sky:
chins lost in the fold
of greatcoat, sheepskin, beard
intent on the tarmac,
as if directions were
scribbled there on the flagstones,
or footprints like dance moves
were etched into the pavement -
how to slide one foot marginally
in front of the other:

They sometimes stop
raise stricken eyes
salute a lone disappearing thought
before they tuck themselves, once again,
back into their necks and hobble on.
There, but for luck,
there, but for sheer tenacity
there, but for whatever reason – go us.
But something in me reciprocates
falls into step with their
laboured tread and uneasy gait,
folds unfelt arms around them,
hologram hug, a useless embrace.

Question…

And what if there isn't any
solace,
what if every word is meaningless
repelled in slow motion
to drop and bounce on the earth
bounce again and spring away
the grass choked with broken sentences
orphaned vowels, stranded words.
What if the light stays dark,
if all moves as through a sluggish dusk,
and everything and all is ash?
Who then will wait for understanding?
Who then will challenge life?
Not I.
Rather let me only walk
and in walking
put at least purpose
there, one step
then another
and so on...

An Occupation

Stationed here,
throwback of some forgotten
watcher,
I bide time;
I spool and unravel her,
weave again and unwind
as the pendulum arcs
mark swathes through the past;
back and further back
scything the dark,
reaping all I've ever known.

Distance outlines you,
so far removed
I can't recall all of you at once
but separate parts, a voice, your eyes
a smile.

Soft the mulch here and heavy
years lined with moss, like graves,
to deaden the drop,
gentle the far reach of pain:
softer still this twilight
a small scuttling of earthen things
crumbling back to the galaxies:
I wait.

Rights

The sun is lying on the
grass, stretched
and pulling the shadows
into the next field, the long yew trees
now spiked and pointing,
shading a ditch all the way
to the dyke's edge.

The gardener has a contraption
for blowing leaves, and every so
often, the same sun
catches an eddy, a whirlpool
of dancing bronze.

Crows gather and wheel by the treetops,
raucous and restless,
stark against a sky
that's more violet than blue,
more silver than grey,
more pearl than matt –
a somewhat reflective ceramic white
and I'll leave it at that.

Before the lacing of tree trunks
a yucca quivers, fine tuning
itself to a pitch, vibrating
like a tuning-fork.

And that, as they say,
places me. Sets the scene –
at least for here.

But, I am light with speculation,
watching the days unfold
and roll themselves out and around
much in the language of ink
a Rorschach test –

*(it could be anything –
but my money is on a crow*)

The odd time I remember why
I'm here, what it is that I have left
and something seizes, abruptly.
Even from here I can catch the same
glimpse of your cheek.
Memories, I have found,
don't always know their place.

Outlook

as we began, we end
mewling for solace:
the milk of human kindness
thinning in the long run
towards change;
background strewn with
shed skin, earlier reinventions
of our same selves.
The inevitable road,
revisited and remembered,
inborn sense of
transience, and in spite of ourselves,
hope.
In the end
its every man for himself,
every woman, failed,
every single child, sold out.

Nemesis

for Noel

You do your best
as son,
you, your mother's son,
as brother to the lost,
scholar, almost priest, teach:
protector of all things just.
Husband and father,
role model for the musketeers
and the thousands that were shaped by
your insight, moulded in the dramatic,
uplifted by your song,
unwittingly touched by your verse.
She arrives, a dawn long ago,
the mauve muse, steals a few breaths, leaves
a nodule of hurt in the vein.
It shows up years later in the angiogram,
impediment against excess, or wayward
influx of the riotous.
Your gaze rolls and drips over these drumlins,
ownership of the curlew's call
the slow unfurling of a fern.
The diameter of your reach, reduced
lungs intake shallowed
but always, always, the light in you
blinding

Future

It’s so big,
we no longer discuss it.
Horrified,
we’re aware it grows,
tumour:
blood diverts, darts away
a shoal of something
pointed.
Knife-edged we grind teeth
chew nails to the quick,
hyper, even in sleep.
Shoulders round
lips permanently thin and
in this quiet dread,
silence suppurates like a sore,
hope leaches
and a terrible static
builds under the skin.
This is fear,
the lid’s off the jar,
despair loose,
our lives unravelling.

Future Take Two

Soon, hunger will take care
of the need to diet;
we'll come to recognize
everything as tat...
and our lives will diminish,
we'll shrink to the size
of our need
a whole, hard potato,
as the world still tilts
on its green fiscal axis.
Our dreams will get too lonely
in our big empty heads
and we'll relocate them
a handspan away from our eyes:
something to smile about
to ourselves
on long bus journeys,
or in thc quict ticking
of our tedious lives

Return

Came the day she stopped
looking
quit the short walk in the evenings
the long look off into the birchwood
sparse branches arching over:
the dark,
deepening away.
That evening
everything fell by the wayside,
hope wilted and died,
drooped over the edges of her life
shrivelled into papery fronds
littered about like curled mulch;
crisp whispers where she walked.
Came the day she stopped
altogether
sat by the window
gave herself up
breaths bled ripe with regret;
came the indigo night
and found her

Even Keel

this pelting rain:
unsettled, uneasy, unquiet
thing, full of static and
dark noise
riding the wind
bombarding tarmac and brick
full tilt through the trees
is snatched and flung
to pummel window and door
beseeches the cracks, implores and
whimpers to be let in,
in… let me in!

They accommodated. Jigsawed.
Slotted time and want and needs
neatly. Courted an alliance,
dallied a degree of affinity,
sequenced esteem. Mutual,
habitual, ritual, liable.
Even keel.
Now, the recall snags, frets like
the bruised remnant of a sore.
The wild rain strains, wrenches
free to fly unbound to an unseen,
but radiant, moon.

Gathering

Near gale force winds waken me
link me to mortality
cries or echoes or maybe even memories
lost across the greatest of divides.
My hold on you -
your hold on the world -
our speck of dust existence to the stars.
In this prevailing moment
a great churning of the cosmos
all lives petering out among the debris,
super nova, dying...dead.

Element

the days pour away
fluid, sand like
a whole river, a desert.
Sometimes I myself am all water
upright and streaming
rivulets coursing
or windscooped grains
shaped
sifting

I wrote of you once
rushing the air,
a blonde child charging.
Somehow, you've made it
abstracted yourself
to imbue everywhere with
an absence I breathe
but can't contain

Rhombus

for Sandra

the woman draws her own breath,
summons lungs' expanse of air
inhales the past, breaks breath of now
drawing deep;
pausing, while air gathers
courses through diaphragm and
breast bone, releases
to sing in her shoulders
hum the length of her
fingertips

I wonder what she sees
this woman, this waif
forehead kissing the wall,
eyes closed, feet bare, earthed to the tile.
Can she sense the fleeting beings
of the past, hundreds of life forms,
the echoing wake,
fluttering shift -
aura overlapping aura, overlapping.

Or is it only this she's aware of, the
inner chant of the blood,
an extension of thought, a pulse
almost tangible, almost touch,
brush invades wall, wall space and so on:

soft strokes burn
ambiguous ...
and the room lies plundered.

there is only the sound of the walls reeling
the dark chalk’s dance on the board
rhythm of marks lacing the walls spine:
a burrowing of surface
the rupture of all things quiet.

I know I felt humbled
envied fusion of mind and body and matter,
felt a whole heart’s breath of want and
that fluttering shift of blessing,
blessed.

Some Say God

After a series of paintings 'Ex Nihilo' by Anne Harkin-Petersen

1. *Awaiting*

Some say god.
An infinite chasm, I think; dark
though darkness had yet to be named,
no light either, nor matter,
just flux and smoke,
caught in an iris, churning.
For how long it roiled there,
who can say?
There was no time, no where,
only there,
and being only there, it Was.

2. *Conception*

Who cannot be aware of the immaculate,
borne holier by an untouched cleansing
the womb in which a world begat,
lamb. Myth created, man.
Primordial shift, time's tilt,
what blueprint, purpose or resolve
compromised expanse?
A particle born broke free, broke again
and so - behold, The Waltz.

3. ***Womb***

Reduction, reaction.
War and all its factions.
the expanse swallowed
intake of deepest breath
held
and the maw of existence widened.
In the half blink of an eyelid
space devoured,
universe became:
Cosmos?

4. ***Charge***

Through the smallest vent
the world inflated
arranged itself
interacted,
flounced fiery skirts,
nuclei lace,
tempestuous rush, force fields
and gravity, born, stole among them
to Create.

5. ***Borne***

Intense
heat gives way to light
energy and mass colliding,
turbulence
none the less creating, violent
clouds retch dust and particle,
split the spherical, gas producing
spewing matter: this spiralling -
be astonished,
creates the endless galaxies!

6. ***Wave***

Bloodlink, blueprint.
That same carbon vein.
Spellbound and caught,
aeons and light years away
we howl to a twinkling dark
finger printed, pock marked moon
our DNA shared,
our genetic song
a chorus for the universe,
in tune with a billion stars.

Cloud

Light daubs the trees
silvers the waving ivy wear:
clump of dark feathered trunk.

The day sits on the fence
a gray pearl, balanced
towards neither rain nor respite.

Timedregs of the hourglass.
All waiting our turn while
blunted memories dissipate

scatter to an old wind
ripe with the scent of hope,
as insistent as all the hands

that have ever touched us.
These have left their mark,
the ravelled mind, the unseeing eye.

Contract

Age inures us;
year by year, cell by stretched cell,
we lay down another skin
against various temptations,
against loss in all its guises,
against pain.

It never works.
At best it blunts the edge
of innocence,
takes the hunger
from our want;
slows our conquering heart.

At worst it raises the bar
of annoyance
makes us doubt
our own potential, our worth,
stifles growth,
dulls an appetite for life.

Age insulates us
then allows us to watch impassively
while we're broken
down, slowly from the inside out
embracing illness as a purpose
a silver-lined opus.

Age isolates us
Lets us sit and reminisce
while our minds cave in
and the pendulum clock
in the long empty hall
goes tick tock tick

Age inures us;
and our world dwindles
to the stretch of a room,
the lie of our bed,
the reach of our hand,
a breath, warm

Guest

Your threshold draws its own line.
But I have followed you
beyond, into a darkened hallway
where breaths bead against a wall
where single words hover, spit, arc,
frazzled by-products of a storm.
Here night is its kindest.
Moonbeams refract through opaque
glass and your face is all mottled
light - innocence caught.
Voices. Yet none of us are really here.
Your whole life passes,
relentless.
Before you can look upwards, or raise a hand to
reach, or close your eyes,
I leave.
Regrets spill out the door before me,
tumble headlong towards the dark, lost.

Cosmic Collective

for Anne

I am an extension of your
arm, the distance
your blue eye can see,
that next thought in your mind.

You are my exhaled breath,
that word on the tip of my tongue,
the next step after the rest.

We are the depth in the painting
the unwritten line in the poem
that silence, just after the song.

Steel

all in all
I admire those females
who can fold
under,
up or into:
those who can crumple
deliciously against a waiting
shoulder,
those who can lean, languishing
towards an offered muscled forearm.
But - to fall asunder among a group
of women –
that is strength

Missing

She has arrived here
by way of all lost things,
innocent, jaded,
so naïve she feels
there couldn't possibly be a past,
that time began here, now,
that all this history
is a lie.

How nice, they tell her,
to have been someone's someone,
to have loved and lost, yes.
Talk then of the economy,
ruin, how one might yet
take an allotment, grow things.

Alone it's easy to forget;
build the wall a little higher
each time surround yourself
with platitudes of brickwork,
circlets of the unbending truth,
know strength in distancing
yourself from others,
find solace in not being present at all.

Polished Stones

1.
Tossed aside, dark
ruby mass; out of context
beating for no-one

2.
Sigh. A thousand sighs.
Sad notes kiss off the dead chords,
the spirit, weeping.

3.
Time passes, tears stop: Hope
leaves your vocabulary.
You look, but don't see.

4.
Magpie. On its own.
Harbinger of the sorrows,
lured by glint of tear

5.
Magpie, monochrome.
Hides purple, indigo, jade,
iridescent poof!

6.
Lonely and listless:
Nevertheless, applauding life.
A breeze…the leafs' rise.

7.
Something shifts. At last.
The world has righted itself;
Offers you the Sun.

8.
The lake lures the moon
shavings and shards fall-
elderflowers froth

9.
I had forgotten.
The lungs full breath, the skins' heat.
Nothing feels like love.

10.
Now, not one breath goes
unnoticed: Before you came
whole decades were lost!

Calm

Words float,
phrases get caught in a loop,
sentences loom.
From this new found state of *equilibrium*
I am all reflective,
all sense of urgency gone
dissipated, the tide
waning, spellbound and spurned by the moon.

It's a stark rationale
no desires,
though neither that sense of despair,
only an inbred keening in the bone
only memory, monochrome
and time with its sidereal air.
The origins of the echo swells -
out of range and a whole other dimension short.

Faith

These things sustain me,
banks of barbed and saffron blare of whin,
white fuzz and buzz of gentle haw,
dogwood of claret red
and posies of primrose coin.
Unsurpassed, the silent lined-up trees
of twisting trunks and
bristling little turrets reach
to point the day in never-ending praise.

Shaman

I am older than flight.
I am the first bronze feather
outlined against a faint sky
camouflaged against the earth.
I am fur and skin,
stone and the rushing tide.
I am thorn and bramble,
moss on the drumlins' curve,
the risen vein in every underside of leaf.
I am the whisper and the scream,
the gasped breath,
and always, the ominous, watchful eye.

Heather Brett

was born in Newfoundland, Canada, and brought up in Ballymena, Co Antrim, Northern Ireland.
She has been living in the South of Ireland since 1984 and Cavan for the past 26 years. Heather is an Arts Facilitator and has been Writer-in-Residence for counties Cavan, Louth and the Midlands Collaboration of Westmeath, Longford, Offaly and Laois.
Founder and Editor of Windows Publications since 1992, Heather has edited over 40 anthologies, with emphasis on promoting younger writers.
'Witness' is her fourth collection.

www.windowspublicationsanddesign.com